Your Free Gift

I wanted to show my appreciation for your purchase so I have put together a free gift for you!

Easy to follow Focus Factor Exercise Summary

Just visit

http://newwheelpublishing.com/FocusFactor/

to download it now

I know you'll love this Gift.

Thanks!

Allen Donaldson

Now Available:

To Do List Mastery: A Stress-Free Guide To Quickly Increase Your Productivity And Get More Done In Less Time
[http://bit.ly/ToDoListMastery]

And

The To Do List Mastery Journal
[http://bit.ly/TDLMJournal]

Build your success on a daily basis. Easily master your tasks and feel a sense of accomplishment as you become more productive day by day.

Here are some of the reviews:

"It's a really great book for those who are feeling overwhelmed and stressed and I really think that it truly provided me with some value. It was exactly what I needed today." – Maxie

"Love the 80/20 Approach to 'To Do lists.' Prioritizing the highest leverage tasks to make the most impact. Can't wait to implement these principles..." – Dip

"The to do list templates and step by step guidance were very helpful for taking the first step. I am taking solid steps for creating a more efficient cycle of time during my day." - Andres

Contents

Chapter 1: Building a Rock-Solid Routine

Recognizing areas of your life that need improvement means work to find solutions to the problems lurking there. One great way to change the path you are on is to implement positive routines that become ingrained. These routines then guide you to better decisions and make your overall life satisfaction higher.

It takes work, practice, and sometimes many incidences of sliding into old or bad habits. That's part of the process. You then can start working to get back on track to find the success and the realization when you build these positive routines into your daily life. Still, this is a very possible life change if approached in the right way.

Athletes are a great example of why successfully establishing routines can change your life. Athletes recognize the need for preparation in every way possible so that timing is ideal, actions happen at the right time and the desired end result on the track, court, or field is achieved.

Routines are a healthy way to ensure all the steps to a particular goal are done in the right order and without taking up a significant portion of the decision-making part of the brain. For athletes, this means the difference between a successful play or game and an unsuccessful one. If the routine is not firmly cemented in their basal ganglia, the pattern is not recognized and not completed. One second is all it can take for that routine to be thrown off and the end result compromised. This is a huge reason why athletes believe in and utilize routines as much as possible.

Routines for different times, such as practice, pre-competition, and post-competition encourage the individual to be prepared for the tasks ahead in every way possible. The consistency of the same routine can be calming and help the individual focus on the task at hand and minimize any distractions that try to encroach on their focus.

Likewise, for you it can be important to set routines for the morning, throughout the day and even before bed to ensure you optimally reach the success you have set as your desired end result. Various routines can sync together to focus you toward that one ultimate goal. Having the various routines set can also be important because your cues can be in different locations and have the same effect. Facing variety and being able to pick out the important things, like the cues for your positive routines, means you are well on your way to keeping those routines long-term and regardless of the changes to your schedule that you cannot avoid.

The Newest Theory of Motivation and Its Impact on Routine

A new theory of motivation has been introduced stemming from more observation of how we live in our fast-moving society. Currently, the theory of "self-determination" states that humans have a drive to be connected with one another; yet autonomous and self-determined. If this drive is fed, people tend to live more satisfactory lives. Routines are a good way to help with this drive, as they incorporate healthy repetition to your life and give you time and initiative to pursue further goals and dreams after the routines are established and the desired goals are accomplished. Routines also help increase confidence levels because you easily accomplish the goals related to setting and maintaining routines.

The Secret of How Habits Work

Habits, like any other trick or trend in a life, have secrets that help them succeed. Some habits, once you fall into them, include aspects that are hard to break. These tend to be bad habits rather than good habits, unfortunately. The good news is there are three steps involved in successfully ingraining a habit into your daily lifestyle. Likewise, these three steps are important to know if your habits aren't positive and need altered.

The first step is the cue, which lets your brain know there is a specific routine you hope to complete. Next is the routine itself, which requires practice and attention at first until you learn the steps and have them set in your brain. Finally, there is a reward. This can be any positive result at the end of the routine. Your brain will register this positive reinforcement and be more likely to activate the loop this particular routine is set on in your brain for future occasions.

Another part of the success of routines, and the secret to your ability to complete the routines while doing other activities, is the fact that routines are stored in a different part of the brain than the area that makes decisions. The basal ganglia are where patterns are stored, as well as emotions and memories. Meanwhile, the frontal cortex is where you make decisions to complete other actions while mid-routine, i.e. driving and changing the radio station simultaneously.

The key to implementing successful routines is also laid out in a clear manner known as the three R's.

These are:

Reminder – This sets you up for the start of the routine. It lets you know it will begin and triggers the patterns that are set into your basal ganglia.

Routine – This is the set of steps itself. It can be whatever routine you have found suits you. It does not need to be complex or even lengthy. It simply needs to suit you and be the predetermined positive routine you are hoping to use for the long-term.

Reward – This is the part that tells your brain that it wants to repeat this routine. This lets you know you got something good and want to get that reward again.

Similar to what is discussed above, there has to be an original trigger, followed by the routine itself and the resulting benefit for you. This further cements the process in your synapses and ensures you can keep the habit and routine, making them a regular part of your future.

How Does All This Impact Rock-Solid Routine Creation?

Knowing how to create habits is the best place to start with creating a routine. The better grasp you have on the steps required to ingrain a habit mean you can better imprint a new, positive routine into your lifestyle. Setting reasonable goals is a part of the process to create those new habits and routines. Therefore, like athletes, now you can better understand the importance of routines and the higher levels of success with well-crafted routines.

Chapter 2: Coping with Distractions and Instant Gratification

One thing that impacts all aspects of our lives is distraction. These distractions take away from productive time at work and are a huge factor in not completing a list of tasks you face at home. They can be innocent, like the well-meaning call or visit from a friend, to the ever-present and notable distraction of Internet and other forms of entertainment that draw you in and make you forget your previous good intentions to clean, organize, or complete another specific project.

One way to avoid distraction is to create a schedule, use a calendar app and force yourself to stick to that schedule. If you take this approach, be sure to schedule all the important things, like chores that need done regularly, activities that cannot be missed and even eating – if this is something you tend to forget.

Scheduling your life in this way, for a set amount of time at least, can help you avoid distractions and also avoid falling back into the bad habits or negative routines that have gotten you to the point where you find change is necessary. If this is the case, scheduling the basics is your way to creating the new, positive routine and helping your life change to follow that routine.

Make It A Game

Instant gratification is a problem in today's society, where food can be attained in mere minutes and communication worldwide can be instantaneous. With this in mind, it makes sense that most of us have issues creating positive routines because they take longer to show their successful impact.

Instead, allow yourself some harmless diversions that take away from the need for instant gratification by providing entertainment. Time yourself while doing chores or boring tasks, or find a way to make a game out of the remaining portion of a task at hand. This diverts your attention from the need to get the task done while still allowing you to complete said task when you want/need to get it done.

Employing these methods help you find success with your main goals of creating new, positive routines while allowing for a bit of diversified attention to let you think you are going slightly off-task. Sometimes this is the difference between success and giving up short of the finish line.

Avoid Multitasking

I know, above it tells you to give yourself smaller tasks, like timing yourself, to get a task completed. This, however, is not the same as trying to complete two tasks or two portions of a routine simultaneously. If you attempt to multitask, you take away focus from both tasks and neither task is done efficiently. It is also twice as difficult to finish the task at hand, because you have split yourself between two. Instead, take half the time and complete one task, then focus completely on the other in order to be efficient and help ingrain these parts of a new routine into your basal ganglia.

It has been shown that multitasking, instead of allowing you to get more done in a shorter amount of time, actually doubles the time each task takes to complete, compared to what would be necessary if you do the tasks one at a time. Therefore, stick to one thing at a time and move onto the next task in the time that would have been taken up by your multitasking.

Chapter 3: How to Make Your Morning Work – It Sets Up Your Entire Day

The way you approach the start carries over into the success of the entire time span of that day.

There are some reliable methods to creating a successful morning routine. While having a cup of coffee can be helpful with that initial caffeine boost, that may not be a benefit in the long-term when your body rebels on the days you try to skip your coffee or simply don't have time to fit it in. Therefore, stick to routines that get your mind and body active with minimal "cheats."

A healthy breakfast is a great way to start the day. Giving yourself time to make the breakfast, sit down for a reasonable amount of time and eat. It gives you time to wake up and prepare for the various tasks ahead. Yes, this can even be time to grab that cup of coffee for those who can't live without it. Granted, this too is a routine that may not be possible every day. However, looking after your health is a great goal to work into positive routines. Therefore, eating a healthy meal to start your metabolism and give your mind time to kick into top gear is a worthwhile routine to put into action.

Another possible morning routine that can help set your day on the right track is exercise. Yoga can be a great addition to a morning routine, while a morning jog or even walk can get the blood pumping and help set a positive mood with the endorphins created.

If exercise isn't an ideal start to your day, there is always an exercise of the mind. Meditation can be helpful to get your thoughts in order and dispel any negative vibes that might be brewing. You can awaken ideas and plans while organizing your mind and feel refreshed before tackling the work or home-related tasks ahead.

It can also be helpful to spend a set amount of time reviewing the goals you have set, the progress you feel you have made toward those goals and any adjustments you have found will be necessary in your efforts to find success. This is a great way to get your mind working and positively focused in the morning, especially if you are more goal-oriented compared to exercise or relaxation motivated.

How Goal Setting Really Works

In order to set goals that are within the realm of possibility to achieve, it is best to approach the goal setting process with logic and tried and true methods.

SMART goal setting is one great method to ensure you are setting goals that will benefit you in the long-term, rather than impeding your efforts to reach success.

SMART goal setting provides five qualifications for the goals to be set. These qualifications ensure you are within the realm of pushing your boundaries in a reasonable manner.

SMART goals are:

Specific – Setting a goal that can be measured makes it easier to attain. Setting goals that have a specific end point are also important. Therefore, try to ask the questions who, what, when, and how to see if your goal can be explained in a specific way.

Measurable – Having a way to see progress is important in any attempt to complete a goal. If possible, have points you can achieve en route to the big goal, like a number of minutes spent exercising that can be gradually increased, pounds lost or other measurable points along the path to success.

Attainable – Goals need to be something within your scope of possibility. Don't set the goal of being an Olympian in an event you have never experienced yourself. Likewise, don't set goals that will take more money or time than you have available.

Relevant – Make the goal something that will enrich your life as it currently stands. Make it a step toward a larger goal to improve health or quality of life. Make goals that will set good examples for others. Do not set goals to make others happy, however. Instead, focus on things you will feel success at accomplishing for yourself.

Timely – Set deadlines that fit with the scope of the goal. Don't expect a multi-step, complex goal to be completed in a few days or a week, but likewise do not give yourself a year to complete something that can be finished in a month's time.

Another idea is to start small and simple. Work your way up to the complex, really challenging goals and routines that you aspire to have. No one started out with the really tough stuff. Everyone apprentices first. Likewise, goals and routines in your personal life can't just be laid out in a complex domino pattern and followed with immediate success.

Making Goal Setting Part of Your Routine

Making goal setting part of your routine is an easy task to accomplish. Simply consider goal setting one of the first steps of the routine. The goals can be focused on the tasks that need accomplished during the routine, or they can be focused toward long-term successes. Either way, incorporating the creation of goals into the routine means you are thinking about all aspects of the process and connecting them. This is a great way to ensure a routine gets implemented successfully. The more you focus on it and weave it into the workings of your life, the better your chances are to be successful and find happiness with your life filled with positive routines.

Goal setting can be a regular appointment for yourself. You can sit down once a week or once a month, if a daily goal setting is unnecessary. This still allows you to keep yourself on your desired path and realize how close you are getting to achieving certain goals so that new goals can be set. This is a very helpful process while attempting to change habits and instill positive routines. It shows you that things are working and allows you to tweak your routine or the tasks you have set for yourself to help you get closer to the success you desire.

Chapter 4: Finding focus

Finding focus while establishing new routines can be difficult. There are some tips that can be helpful in this endeavor.

1. Set up a space where distractions aren't welcome

If your goals revolve around work time, your office should be a distraction free zone. If this is more related to home tasks or things done outside the office, designate the kitchen, the dining room table or wherever you are comfortable as the area where distractions can't reach you. This helps you focus on your tasks and lets others know not to bother you when you are in that certain room. Make sure to have all Internet-connected devices and televisions off in that particular area so as to avoid those time-stealing activities.

2. Meditation can be helpful when the day gets overwhelming

Not only can meditation help get you off on the right foot in the morning, but it can also be an activity to employ during a break when things seem to be too much to handle. Have a few short exercises handy or even just a picture that can be your escape destination. Close your eyes and picture that location and you in that spot, relaxing for a few minutes. After your short "vacation," you can get back to the task at hand feeling a bit refreshed.

3. Leave time for breaks – and take them

Meditation and other relaxing activities are difficult when you are mid-task and stressing. Breaks actually increase productivity by giving your brain and body time to relax mid-task. This helps you conserve energy to finish out the day's list of to-do's and hopefully won't leave you completely exhausted at the end. Completion of routines and tasks is easier to accomplish if you fit in a break or three during the course of the day. Make sure if you promised yourself a break, you do take that break and remove yourself from the situation for a few minutes.

4. Keep track of distractions, so they can be addressed when they become a regular issue.

You may think a particular thing happens once in awhile. If you are dealing with a lot of distractions, write down what they are and how often they occur. You may realize that one particular distraction or a small group of distractions are the main things that prevent you from completing your tasks. If this is the case, addressing those issues can free up a significant amount of time and help you get back to the routines you are hopefully making a long-lasting part of your more successful life.

5. Set limits and be strict about keeping them

Some distractions, i.e. situations that crop up and need addressed immediately; cannot be avoided. If this is the case, then set a five-to-10 minute time limit to discuss and resolve these situations. Once that time is up, shut down the conversation and return to your work. This means higher success rates for both tasks.

Chapter 5: Super-Charge Your Self-Control (why its like a muscle and can be strengthened)

Most people find their biggest weakness is saying yes when they should say no. This is where valuable time is lost doing work for others and slacking on your own, giving advice when you should be working and otherwise focusing on anything, but what you need to be focused on. Now is the time to super-charge your self-control.

There are some rules that can benefit anyone with less than exemplary self-control. Putting these rules into action can help strengthen that self-control and put you in a better place to handle potential issues in the future.

1. Learn to say No.

Saying no to others is a significant problem, but it particularly comes to light when attempting to create better routines in your life to lead a more fulfilling existence. Too often, people strive to pacify everyone around them and their life is the area that suffers the most. Learn that saying no to people is not being mean or selfish. It helps you focus on the important things in your life, it gives you more time for family and the hobbies or enjoyable activities that help you stay rounded and content. Saying no just means you have priorities. People do appreciate that, although that is not readily apparent when you first say no and have previously always said yes.

2. Set Available and Unavailable time each day

This goes along both with giving yourself time to take a break and saying no to people. If you have times set aside during the day when you are unavailable, stick to those. Those times can be your break times or times you work hardest on a project that is nearing deadline. Either way, if you are unavailable, people cannot distract you and draw your time away from a task that needs concentration and your entire effort.

3. Separate the Critical Thinking and Routine Tasks and act Accordingly

On days when stress is getting to you or your brain is taxed, choices that should be simple require more time. There are ways to deal with these routine tasks that occur each day (choosing lunch, for example). One option is to have a fallback choice. If it's a rough day, have one choice that you know is available and never out of season. This can be your response when you look at choosing lunch as a mountain that can't be scaled. Another option is to face these tasks ahead of time, in times when your focus isn't stretched between important issues in a business meeting or troubleshooting a project that needs turned in ASAP.

Meanwhile, critical thinking tasks require your time and focus. These tasks should be given an appropriate time block in your day and not rushed through in downtime between scheduled tasks. These tasks need to be faced when you are running on all cylinders and capable of the smart decisions that need to be made for critical thinking tasks. This means your self-control stays intact and the appropriate levels of focus are used on the various tasks ahead of you.

4. Be Flexible with your Expectations

Don't immediately expect success with no issues. Understand you are going to find some problems with your plans and be ready to adjust as necessary. No one jumps from point A to point Z without a few stops along the way. Knowing that things are going to end differently than what you think is going to happen and being prepared to roll with the changes is a great show of flexibility. This can be a benefit in countless other aspects of your life as well.

5. Rely on your Emotions

Letting your heart make decisions is a good way to ensure

your self-control improves. Your head sometimes overcompensates to make those decisions look good to others. Your heart remembers the important details that make or break your life. Listen to your heart when it looks like self-control is failing.

6. Remember What is Important

When your self-control becomes an issue, take a moment to remember the things that are important in your life. Your family, your career and personal successes, the things you hope to accomplish – these are all reasons to have strong self-control and avoid situations where that can be challenged. Keep them in mind when you feel a potential problem arise.

Chapter 6: Important Tricks for Success in Your Positive Routines

There are some important things to keep in mind while trying to implement positive routines. These are great things to consider when the attempt gets overwhelming or things seem to stagnate without new progress attained.

Getting Unstuck

When implementing a new routine, it is logical that some steps won't work as smoothly as you first expect. If this is the case, there are ways to use creative thinking and get unstuck from that particular point that doesn't jive with other aspects of your routine.

1. Look at the issue head-on

Be honest about what the problem is with the place you got stuck. Is it too difficult or do you simply lose interest? Are there ways to salvage this point in the routine? If not, it's time to try another tactic.

2. Create a list of viable options that still can progress logically to the next step in the routine

Routines work best when the entire process goes smoothly

and follows a logical progression. Therefore, if your current routine has one point where you get stuck repeatedly, that point needs replaced. However, the replacement activity must still logically move on to the next step in the process. You wouldn't step from the shower to run to the grocery store in your towel. You would dry off, get dressed and then put on shoes and grab keys before heading to the car.

Likewise, the steps you choose must have some logical progression to help you ingrain your routine into your daily activities so you can complete it with minimal thought and mental effort on your part.

3. Try out one (or more) of these options

Once you have an idea of some options to change the order or your routine or replace that one sticking point, try them out. Like the first effort, you won't know what works and what doesn't without trying it out.

4. Evaluate the results

Here again, it is time to step back and look honestly at your routine. Is it accomplishing what you hoped it would? Did you lose something along the way? Did you gain something? It's a great opportunity to let yourself know what is working and what isn't while it's still new. Then the necessary changes can be made while things are still in a learning phase.

5. Keep the step or skip it altogether

Sometimes you can save the point in the routine when you get stuck. Sometimes, that step can simply be eliminated and a smooth transition from the step before directly to the step after can be accomplished. You are the only one that can accurately determine this.

Build in time for mental renewal

It is always important to factor in time for mental renewal. When giving your brain new information and expecting it to sink in, it is a good idea not to overload the brain and give it some time to fully process and retain the new information. Therefore, you should give yourself a break between starting new routines. Give yourself a set time to fully learn the routine you are starting. Once that seems to be a success, give yourself a week to just tackle life's tasks and enjoy the success from implementing a positive routine. Then, if you have a list of changes you are set on making, move onto the next routine you hope to change.

Don't Give Up

Consider the fact that you took a lot of time building up all of your bad habits or routines that don't help you move forward and improve your quality of life. If these took years to put in place, you can't simply overturn them and have new and better routines take hold in a day or three. Therefore, it may get hard and you may have one – or several – instances where you fall into the old routine. Take a step back, consider the areas that need work or increase the incentive to do better and get back at completing the new routine.

This will help you move forward with the routine and change that aspect of your life and many others. Hard work and determination go far in this situation and many other important life events. Therefore, it is important to not give up once you commit to creating and implementing positive routines. This was a choice you made to improve your life. Keep that in mind, as well as any other incentive that will kick you back in the right direction when you go astray.

Chapter 7: Famous People with Successful Routines

There are countless people throughout history, beyond athletes, who have found routines to be the key to reaching and maintaining success in their lives. These people are typically creative, like writers or artists. Despite the idea that creativity is random and unpredictable, these individuals have found that to be far from true. A bit of direction can make all the difference in being creative on a regular basis and being able to cultivate financial success from that creativity – at least in the case of writers.

There are also many great leaders who found their routines to be vital when attempting to lead a nation or enact significant changes in the government or other large areas of a country's leadership and justice systems.

Winston Churchill

Winston Churchill had an intriguing morning routine. Churchill awoke at 7:30 a.m. yet he remained in his bed until 11 a.m. He ate breakfast in bed, read his mail, and perused the papers available. Then, he did work, dictating to secretaries from the comfort of his bed. At 1 p.m. each day, he enjoyed a three-hour lunch with his family and visitors. Then he retired to his office for two more hours of work. Churchill also worked for an hour after dinner, which was reportedly the highlight of his day.

These routines for Churchill ensured he did the amount of work required to become the famed statesman we now learn about from history books. His contributions to the United Kingdom cannot be ignored.

Stephen King

Stephen King became a famous author, penning thousands upon thousands of words and hitting the bestseller charts again and again with the help of his routines. One of his routines is the way he addresses his writing; he begins at a certain time and has a specific thing to drink while he is writing. This helps him focus on the process of creating a new work.

Fred Rogers

Remember Mister Rogers' Neighborhood? That is a prime example of routine at its best. Every child for years knew exactly how the day would go, from Mister Rogers coming in the door and changing into his sweater and sneakers. The sheer comfort of knowing the show from start to finish and yet still having new experiences and learning new things taught countless children manners, letters, and other vital information.

Fred Rogers himself had routines he carried on throughout his life, including a habit of swimming daily that continued through his 70's. The man had certain expectations and beliefs, values that were consistent and well-known. This man is a great example of how routines can make your life exemplary and have an impact for many years on countless others around you.

Emily Dickinson

Emily Dickinson was known for her writing. However, she had a very strict routine that she followed while attending Mount Holyoke. That schedule had strict times to rise, eat breakfast, study, eat lunch, have silent study time and practice for piano and other pursuits. This schedule probably prepared her well for later in life when she had to be her own taskmaster while writing.

Toni Morrison

Toni Morrison is another writer who understands the need for routine, be it conscious or unconscious. Morrison did an interview when she recognized the importance of routines for writers as a prime ingredient that leads to successful creation. Morrison's routine is a morning one, where she gets up and makes coffee before watching the dawn break. This prepares her for the day ahead and her efforts to create on paper the characters that live within her head.

George W. Bush

George W. Bush was the type to tackle the day early, typically arriving at the Oval Office by 6:45 a.m. during his Presidency. He did not spend a significant amount of time on meals, eating quickly and returning to the tasks at hand. However, he made time each day to work out and focus on his physical health.

C.S. Lewis

C.S. Lewis had a particular pattern that worked for him in some situations. It was a pattern he developed in Bookham, Surrey, England where he studied with William Kirkpatrick. In this routine, he was eating breakfast at 8 a.m. and at his desk by 9 a.m. At that time, he would read or write until 1 p.m. Lunch would be served at 1 p.m. during this ideal routine and by 2 p.m., he would be out to walk and talk, preferably with a good friend. Tea should be enjoyed at 4:15 p.m., according to Lewis. From 5 p.m. to 7 p.m., more work should be accomplished. This should be followed by dinner, an evening of light reading and bed no later than 11 p.m. This schedule greatly agreed with Lewis, as it is the one he remembered fondly and wished he could emulate at other locations.

John Grisham

John Grisham set brutal expectations for himself, waking up at

5 a.m. and the requiring himself to write his first word by 5:30 a.m. five days a week. This seems slightly harsh because he expected himself to shower, dress, traverse the five minute journey to his office, pick up a cup of coffee along the way, and sit down with his legal pad to write at the stroke of 5:30 a.m. Grisham also set a goal of writing a page per day. After he found success, however, his routine became much more relaxed.

Charles Darwin

The renowned Charles Darwin began his day at 7 a.m., usually with a walk. After breakfast at 7:45 a.m., he found 8 to 9:30 a.m. to be his best time for work. He took a break for reading letters from 9:30 to 10:30 a.m. Following that, he worked in his study again, largely considering that the end of his workday when he left again at midday. At noon he took another walk, then he had lunch at 12:45 p.m. He rested, took more walks and spent another hour in his study from 4:30 to 5:30 p.m., addressing the final matters for his day. In the evening he rested, had a light high tea and typically spent time with the ladies of the family, playing games like backgammon before he went to bed at 10 p.m.

Thomas Friedman

Thomas Friedman is another individual who enjoys an

energetic start to the day, opting to ride his exercise bike first thing. His day is then filled with busy meetings in the city of Washington, D.C.

John Updike

John Updike thrives by living a very relaxed routine that nonetheless gets him through the day. After breakfast, he works until lunch. However, that work includes both writing and attending to the so-called "junk" in his life, like responding to letters he receives. Updike also notes that having routines is what keeps a lot of writers persevering, rather than opting for other careers with a less creative payoff, but a more reliable pay check.

Mahatma Ghandi

Ghandi awoke each day at 3:30 or 4 a.m. He said prayers twice a day, ate bland food and always spent time both in silence and in avid discussion with visitors. This man also spent time on correspondence regularly. The littlest detail, like the small segment of a pencil he had been using for a significant amount of time, was important to him. He preference for the small pencil segment once caused a strenuous search by his handlers when he refused other writing utensils, waiting instead until his specific pencil segment was found!

Chapter 8: What NOT to do when Creating a Routine

There are some things that you may not think of when you are committed to changing your lifestyle and implementing new, positive routines. Below are some tactics that won't help in the long run if you are set on changing the way you handle life.

1. Don't Get Rid of the Things that Work

You may have already found one or more things that help you be more productive with your daily tasks. Incorporate those into your new routine. Don't get rid of everything you have done in the past, but scrap those things that have not helped in increasing your productivity.

2. Don't Jump in Without a Plan

Starting a new routine needs to be thought out and outlined. Don't jump into the deep end with the complex schedule and no way to get all the tasks set out done. Organization is a good habit to develop while creating and implementing positive routines. This can help you get back on track if you do go astray.

3. Don't Skip Meals to Keep Up with The Schedule You

Set

Eating helps your brain function. Those calories help you recharge for the next steps in the day. Also, the time saved on running out and getting food is minimal, the time spent on ordering into the office or your home is even less. While these may not be the healthiest food options, it is still important to stay fed in order to be able to face tasks with the best weapons available in your mental arsenal.

4. Don't Ignore Your Strengths or the Times You Already Excel

Some people do better in the morning hours. Others excel in the evening. You know when you do the best work, come up with the best ideas or shine the most. Use that to your advantage and plan the tasks that need your best accordingly. Obviously, if you are working with people in other time zones or have other circumstances that prevent this, you need to take those into consideration. However, do the best you can in the time when you typically do that high quality work.

5. Don't sell yourself short

Remember you can do a lot more than you typically give yourself credit for. This is true of many people the world over. Don't set limitations thinking you can't accomplish the harder tasks or aren't ready for more complex issues. Give it your best and see where it goes. You will most likely surprise yourself. It's testing your limits that truly allows you to see you can reach the mountain peak with ease.

Chapter 9: Conclusion

Honing your focus in order to implement positive routines for the long-term takes effort and planning. It takes some work to create new habits that are valuable and help you move forward toward long-term goals.

While you are working toward those goals, it is important to address distractions. Sometimes this means keeping track of them for a certain period to see the biggest pattern of issues and what is needed to combat those distractions. Creating a zone that is distraction-free helps, while other important things to remember are to focus on one task at a time. Multitasking may seem to save time, but it actually increases the time spent on each task and therefore takes up more time than if you had tackled the jobs one at a time.

Eating healthy and sometimes incorporating exercise routines can help get the blood flowing and keep the energy levels high to face a day filled with tasks to accomplish. Set those tasks up so the harder tasks are scheduled for the part of the day when you excel. Meanwhile, learn to schedule tasks that are repetitive and yet sometimes take up far too much of your time for in the evening hours while you are winding down. Or, if that isn't feasible, have go-to options for the days when choosing your lunch or your outfit would be far too difficult on top of all the other time-consuming tasks you have ahead of you.

Maintaining self-control is extremely important while trying to keep your focus and fine-tune positive routines. Remember what is important to you – family, goals, long-term results – and then focus on these things in your life when someone doesn't appreciate you saying no to them.

Like any other major changes you are trying to implement, the creation of new routines through focus and effort takes time and will involve some minor slipping into old habits. Be prepared for this and keep pushing through. Take a look at what points seem to be the biggest issue and determine if those points of the routine need changed or can simply be skipped without major upheaval in the overall routine.

Finally, it is very important to incorporate successful tactics into the new routine. Don't scrap everything you have previously done, thinking a new start will magically allow you to find success. If something already works, keep it for the new routine. You can gain confidence by already having areas where you know you will be successful.

Many creative minds throughout history have found success by creating routines and sticking to them. Some of them opted for exercise to start the day, while others prefer a quiet start enjoying the sunrise or addressing correspondence. Either way, they found what worked for them and stuck to it. This is the key to success for you as well.

For those days when things are difficult, remember that Winston Churchill worked in bed until just before lunch, or that John Grisham had high expectations for himself that he met during the work week. This allowed him to leave his job as a lawyer and become the fulltime writer we know of today. Finally, think of Fred Rogers, whose daily routine became a staple in the lives of generations of children and helped them learn important values that they pass on to their children even now.

Your Free Gift

I wanted to show my appreciation for your purchase so I have put together a free gift for you!

Easy to follow Focus Factor Exercise Summary

Just visit

http://newwheelpublishing.com/FocusFactor/

to download it now

I know you'll love this Gift.

Thanks!

Allen Donaldson

Enjoyed this book?

Thank you so much for your support!

If you enjoyed this book, I'd be grateful if you'd post a short review on Amazon. Your support really does make a difference and I read all the reviews personally so I can get your feedback and make this book even better.

I would love to hear from you because I really value your support, feedback and insight so I can better serve you in the near future.

Thank you so much!

Allen

www.ingramcontent.com/pod-product-compliance
Lightning Source LLC
Chambersburg PA
CBHW051259170526
45165CB00004B/1776